GALAXY LOVE

For information about permission to reproduce selections from this book,
write to Permissions, W. W. Norton & Company, Inc.,
500 Fifth Avenue, New York, NY 10110

For information about special discounts for bulk purchases, please contact
W. W. Norton Special Sales at specialsales@wwnorton.com or 800-233-4830

Manufacturing by Berryville Graphics
Book design by Chris Welch
Production manager: Lauren Abbate

Library of Congress Cataloging-in-Publication Data

Names: Stern, Gerald, date. author.
Title: Galaxy love : poems / Gerald Stern.
Description: First edition. | New York : W. W. Norton & Company, [2017]
Identifiers: LCCN 2016046274 | ISBN 9780393254914 (hardcover)
Classification: LCC PS3569.T3888 A6 2017 | DDC 811/.54--dc23 LC
record available at https://lccn.loc.gov/2016046274

W. W. Norton & Company, Inc.
500 Fifth Avenue, New York, N.Y. 10110
www.wwnorton.com

W. W. Norton & Company Ltd.
15 Carlisle Street, London W1D 3BS

1 2 3 4 5 6 7 8 9 0

GALAXY LOVE

POEMS

Gerald Stern

W. W. Norton & Company

Independent Publishers Since 1923

New York | London

For Noah, Lukas, and Jeremy

CONTENTS

ACKNOWLEDGMENTS

Poems in this volume have appeared or will appear in the following journals:

American Poetry Review: "Perish the Day," "Bollingen Ezra Pound, 1949," "Merwin," "Route 29," "Lips," "Billionaires"

Five Points: "Ruby Red," "Main Bridge," "Decades"

Great River Review: "Bastards," "Blue Particles," "Dead Lamb"

Massachusetts Review: "Lips," "Silence"

Miramar: "Cup Cake Store," "Bess, Zickel, Warhol, Arendt," "Bollingen Ezra Pound, 1949"

Poetry: "Loneliness"

The Progressive: "Coal Barons"

Santa Clara Review: "The Truth," "The Hill"

Slab: "Grandfathers," "Song of Deborah," "Blue Jay," "Ich Bin Jude"

Smartish Pace: "Dark Blue Geese," "Ritsos," "Bohème," "KGB, The Reading"

Tin House: "Book of the Dead," "Visit from Mars," "Hamlet Naked"

Some of these poems were included in the chapbook *Perish the Day*, published by Miramar Editions, edited by Christopher Buckley and Gary Young.

Cover painting, titled *Rookery* (2014) by Louise Fishman, courtesy of Cheim & Read gallery.

GALAXY LOVE

The Truth

The truth is
I'd rather it were a piebald than my green Honda
though what I really want is the 1950 Buick
with the small steering wheel and the strip in the window
and the cigar lighter in the back seat
and a tasselated handhold
I drove myself to the junkyard,
or the Winslow belonging to one of the browner poets
of Andalucía that lasted twenty-five years.

Just think of the wise conversations with the court mechanic
and the references to Aristotle, he who wrote
in the *Book of Speed* all we have to know
about combustion, he who rode a camel
to the agora every day, the new
three-humped type they bred in Egypt then.

Galaxy Love

There's too little time left to measure
the space between us for that was
long ago—that time—so just lie
under the dark blue quilt and put
the fat pillows with the blue slips
on the great windowsill so we can
look over them and down to the
small figures hurrying by
in total silence and think of the heat
up here and the cold down there
while I turn the light off with the right
hand and gather you in close with the wrong.

Bio VII

Yesterday I was picking at the crumbs,
getting them or not getting them.

Today I am struggling with the worms
so that way you can compare the life of a sparrow
with that of a robin.

I would say I am mostly pulling bodies
out of the ground
and settling down to swallow them alive.

I could talk about two kinds of clouds
or two kinds of shadows I saw in Athens
climbing up a steep and endless hill
with my supper in a bag;
or a pigeon's life in a soft bed,
in an air-conditioned apartment, on a windowsill.

Mostly I was trying to stay awake
so I could eat my sardines in peace
and let my new knowledge take over.
"Visitation" was the name I gave it,
and listened to some American music
before I slept—like the pigeon—for ten hours.

The name was foolish,
time of the Colonels, for Christ's sake.
Ritsos was burying his poems
and swallowing his beautiful pencils.

General Electric was producing tanks
with low-lying cannon
mostly for the knees
just a friendly warning.

Bastards

If you were the bastard it doesn't matter what
the blossoms were nor—if you were a frog—
you could or could not sleep in the azaleas
nor what the fireworks were like in Paris
July 14th, 1950, the first day they turned
the lights on after eleven years; or if you
put her in a taxi afterwards,
not even if you trained to be a doctor
and spread kindness in a hundred places,
not even if you walked all night, not
even cellos mattered, if you were the bastard.

Grandfathers

One of them poured hot lead
into a bucket of cold water so he could
make determinations from the shapes
of the hardened metal for he was chasing
the odd intrusions in a small girl's body;

the other had a small tobacco factory
on the third floor of his house and he engaged
a *Lehrer* for the women there coterminous
with Tampa and Havana though the language was different

so I was only half crazy at the most,
for there was a little sanity in both of them
though more I believe in him with the three floors
than him with only one workable room,
the kitchen and the bedrooms unthinkable,

and I am loyal to the nth degree
whatever *they* would have thought of *me*
and for one of them I would have carried one book,
for another, another.

It's all written down in the steam of my bathroom mirror—
if you can read it.

Bio VIII

Refusing to listen to just any song that comes my way,
playing the mouth organ in homage to Stephen Foster,
soaking my big toe in memory of Libby, left foot,
and reading Hardy, all I ignored out of musical prejudice,
thinking seriously about the foothills north of Tampa, the Alps,
hating the thirty-five-story apartment buildings in South Beach,
always loving the fish sandwiches in Key Largo, the fishermen,
trying to get it straight about Stevens and Hemingway, who
    punched whom,
reading Ezra's chinoiserie for its gossip
thinking Jane Freilicher's eyes are like mine, only mine are
    browner
listening to Bach's Unaccompanied Suites, listening to "Helpless."

Hiphole

As far as the hiphole, every night I dug
into the dirt so I could put my body
partly underground on my long walk from
Lake Garda to Venice and thence to Bologna
and then third class to Florence, for the body
on either side can't rest on a flat surface,
say a wooden floor, but when we slept in
trees we must have slept facedown on top of
a branch and locked our hands to keep from falling
especially if we moved too much in our sleep
for we were monsters then and led alternative
lives with leopard skin of sorts and powerful
tails not to mention sharp teeth for cutting
and jaws for ripping and bird-like claws for holding
on and sometimes for piercing and sometimes just for
flea abatement or simply musing and scratching,
though we had holes too in the crowded forest
close to our trees, surrounded by our bushes,
for we lived mostly in the understories
and that way we left our lakes for distant cities
or what we took for cities then, the thought
was still with us when we were eating
mortadella and warm tomatoes and washing
our faces at the spigots stopping in
the Romanesques to look at the renderings;
we already knew the routes, we had our knapsacks

packed with toothbrushes, dictionaries, sweaters,
and Swiss knives, though we still walked on our knuckles.

Song of Deborah

When she gathered her people
she said "enough of hills" and "stop climbing,"
especially women, especially if you don't want
muscular calves like that
and block the entrances for I will sing you a song of
lush meadows and show you where to plant your
corn, though your tomatoes nearer the tents,
and peppers too, for there will be soups, but in
the meantime I'll start my song for that is
good for breathing, especially at these heights,
and don't look back for you could lose
your balance—after all, you don't have hooves
to jump from rock to rock and, after all,
your babies make you heavy, the poets you carry.

Canticle

"Don't eat the luncheon meats," a friend advised me
but he was talking about his mother's funeral
and not my plan to eat a half a hero at
Leopardi's Pizza near the row of six
young healthy oaks and down the hill from the
larger unpruned tree whose shadow in the
bright March sun I walked and stood on the highest
branch though I was vertical, and the shadow was
flat and on the ground, nor was there a branch to
hold on to and while the sky was empty of clouds—
and blue—and while I was in the tree I ate my
tasteless bread, and meat and cheese, adorned with
tasteless onions and tomatoes, even the
oil was tasteless, even the vinegar,
and I just ate a half, maybe a third,
before I found a wire basket, and such
was food in my little city, Sir Brother Sun,
dear Sister Moon, I had to be desperate.

Miami

Dylan Thomas

Maybe my fiftieth or my sixtieth birthday
awoke to my hearing from harbor and neighbor wood
and the mussel-pooled and the heron-priested shore
though I wasn't the first animal up that day
and someone threw a ten-cent cigar at me,
just what this country needed
and someone surprised me with a chocolate cake
yellow inside, pink at the layers, with two
accusing candles, twisted and edible,
myself to set foot in the still-sleeping town and set forth.

Blue Jay

At least I am luckier than that blue jay
hopping along the bulwark
his rubber leg falling back under him
absolutely doomed, the way it is out there.

My heart goes out to him
though he's more a bully than
any other warm creature that came my way.

I never thought I'd plead for a blue jay
I who haven't pled for seventy years,
I who got on my knees every night
to go through the ritual of my own devising.

I who had no grievances then.

Blue Particles

Don't ever think of Coney Island
where the rabbits once ran wild
or the afternoon we went swimming
though it was only May for we had graduated
and we spent the night eating hot dogs at Nathan's
and took the Screamer back to 96th Street.

Nor should you love too much the white pole
or the long and noisy ride through Brooklyn
the No. 2 that delivered you to your front door
and the Dutch freighter that delivered you to Antwerp,
then the Gare du Nord.

Nor your stubbornness every morning at the small table
and what it was like to walk out into the sunlight
and how the blue particles were your chief influence,
that and the Book of Isaiah
and King Lear rolling in the dirt on Chalk Mountain
the early part of your life.

Ghost

You could have stared all day
and it would rather get more radical than less
or more complex or more fragmental,
chaotic is what I would say,
a rabbit with its own rules,
its nose twitching maybe its ears
the last thing to go
the ears are the last thing to go
the gift of hearing

with no sign of life
neither heart nor lung
but the hearing remains
even if it's like an echo
a tunnel a hole where it goes the ghost goes.

Ich Bin Jude

Who was it threatened to murder
a streetcar full of fucking Nazis in Wien
when he was in the country only two hours
and watched the car empty
including the festooned conductor and the decorated motorman?

The rain wouldn't stop.
The cheapest place in Europe—
September, October, November, 1954.
Your darling city.

Today It's Easter

Today it's Easter and there are black flags over all the porches.
Down the street someone put up an American flag, he
thought it was the 4th of July.
My favorite stores are closed, everyone's at the funeral.

In Disney-Town there is a church that looks a lot
like St. Peter's; and there is a new Pope there,
a woman named Francis.
In the days of Pius her name was Billy.

She is giving a sermon to 900,000 people. In the
sunshine. "Eat what you kill." "Kill what you eat."
"Love what you kill," I forget.

I can't find a black flag for I'm no longer an
anarchist, I'm a liberal radical east coast
socialist prophet-adoring Debs-loving Yid, like him.

The Hill

With me it was the large rat
on the round kitchen table at Della's house
among the crumbs and butter
and I was the terrified one
for he (or she) wouldn't budge.

This was under the letter of love from FDR
for the eight sons serving in World War II
who all came back alive but three or four
bearing scars from the battles in Europe and Asia.

And it was I who drove the Pontiac home
down Roberts Street and past Isaly's
a quarter pound of ice cream for a nickel,
my father in the back seat,
my mother humming "Melancholy Baby,"
going on seventy years now.

Dead Lamb

For some reason there was no more sea,
but there was a *Book of Life* with a roasted lamb
holding a page by means of a cooked onion.

And we were allowed to read a word or two
and since it was a table on Broadway there was
a French dictionary and some bygone novels.

And there were other tables since it was Broadway
and he—the owner—was reading Ernest Gaines
and I undid the rubber bands which held

the dictionary in place plus *Père Goriot*
some other bands and there was a Harry Crews
that crazy man from Florida, it had to be

now thirty years since I saw him at his reading
where he and his wife were talking to each other
and he bent down to kiss her for what he needed

most of all was some kind of reassurance
but I had to hurry down to the river to see
if it had dried up too but there were barges

pushing honeypots north to Albany
and there were two small sailboats flying hither and
whither for water has to go somewhere, in this case,

first to South Amboy, thence to Sandy Hook
for it's downhill from Staten Island south
and water (as Thales said) is the root of everything.

Space and Time

Only fifty minutes away from Filthy Delphos
but there are neither poppy seeds nor strudels
in the reconstructed train station
so Tolstoy had to die unsweetened
and to make matters worse it was now a restaurant
with three people waiting for a table
and by a window, they insisted,
but such is fame that the huge crowd had dispersed
only a century ago, such a short time now,
considering that the bird of paradise
is in charge of time as the crow of space
and what we say is "as the bird of paradise
flies" and it's what we lovers of Tolstoy honor
since the crow is no use to us by land and by sea
for what's the straight line to Filthy Delphos
or for that matter Johnstown or Cleveland Heights
worth in today's by-the-number route?
And you should have seen the glut of people
stretching all the way across the bridge to
New Hope when Harry Truman passed through on his
way to Flemington and New Brunswick and
much earlier Adolf Hitler's good friend Charles Lindbergh
who after all lived twenty miles away as the crow flies
if one hour or more than as the bird of paradise.

Azaleas

There isn't a bee swimming in milk
here, just a perfect recollection of the azaleas
at 23 York next door to the funeral parlor
and what the date was they appeared or when you
first discovered or rediscovered them was
and what their color was or what the word was
and what kind of insects inhabited them
and how the tourists were shocked by the beauty

and what the blessing is for azaleas I would have to ask
Rabbi Diana who has the thick books at her disposal
and I think understands the nature of endless gratitude
and whom I ask to plant something lowly on my hill
when the time comes and not to spend too long
on the Babylonian and to speak for me
and what I love and even to read this,
attested to May 11, 2014, Christian time.

Cup Cake Store

Where their eyes should have been there were only smudges
and where their mouths a kind of thickening
and as for heads they were too small for the bodies
and feet too, the whole thing was foreshortened,
and I could feel the bark coming off as I
looked through the box and there was a patch of red
on the side of the stove which I'm sure was hot to the touch
and there was at least a foot of ice on the river
and saws were everywhere and school was dismissed
so the boys could play hockey with homemade sticks
and the girls could ice skate in their white leather boots
and if I were living then it could have been
the year I broke my leg or when my mother
made me baloney sandwiches so I could join
the tar workers when they sat down for lunch
and cigarettes, Coolidge was still alive,
King George was king, FDR was president.

Perish the Day

It's not just Larry who keeps going to
meetings when there's no one there—I went
to one in the latrine where a body was hanging
from a pipe and a finger had written in vapor
Just a Warning but whoever dragged him in
forgot to take his boots off before or after
and there was only one person there one live
person and he was cleaning the toilet with Ajax the magic
cleanser and he had an Irish accent mixed with
English I myself heard in Scotland
so that makes two when in walks Larry and then
for an hour or more he and Jonathan Swift, the
Ajax man, talked horses and, as Larry said,
an angel disguised as a fly flew into the ear
then into the brain of the horse, you should watch
where you put the swab and you should scratch the smooth skin
closest to the skull so your hand can slip
onto the horse's head which he would shake free
and move along the fence so he could bend down
for new weed and as for the meeting it lasted
just long enough to cut the dead man down and
wash him off but it was hard getting the boots
off without cutting or snipping for
there were no laces that's what I want to say
there were no laces on the day we unhanged him.

Poverty

Poverty I learned from the romance of my grandfather
coming over on steerage with three or was it six
dollars sewn into his vest and he ate
cheap and slept cheaper going from this bed to that and
by the time he was twenty he owned a string
of nickelodeons and at thirty he owned
the Mayflower Hotel in Atlantic City
plus the jitneys on Atlantic Avenue
but lost it all in the postwar depression
except he sewed a fifty-dollar bill
in his favorite vest and from this fresh start
he made a killing on Seventh Avenue
with a dollar bill in every right-hand pocket
the way there was a penny in penny loafers
and I put a twenty under my insole and
one time I had to tear my shoe apart
to pay for my supper the restaurant had the best
sweet potatoes anywhere my favorite vegetable
and Brussels sprouts my other and beets and cauliflower
but I had other shoes and found another
twenty and lived by a river with the birds
so loud in May I had to lock the doors
there were three and I had a table with
papers and dozens of books and sometimes
food and animal figurines, a small
wooden pelican, a glass rabbit, a

clay canary, and on a shelf a Deco
clock, a rooster and two pigs disguised
as salt and pepper shakers and some pots
I bought in Iowa and a photograph
of my parents in their store in Detroit, two
orphans almost in tears and in the next room
thirty-five books I am working with just now
and photos and dishes and manuscripts and candlesticks
and tin roses in a cloisonné vase
and more in the next room where I take my naps
and paintings and two thousand books upstairs
and boxes full of letters and rugs on the floor I
dragged from other continents and though I am rich now
by the old standards I always have a twenty
in one of my heels, usually the left foot and
usually underneath the insole I say
it's there for a rainy day I say it's just
in case I say it's for an emergency
though what it could buy now—not nearly enough
for a straw hat to cover my sunspots.

Bess, Zickel, Warhol, Arendt

Aunt Bess died from forgetting and when I
visited her at her last apartment she kept
asking me if I had eaten and poured
bowl after bowl of Rice Krispies for me though
I might add no banana, no milk
no sugar and most of all, no spoon.

And Zickel, my bewildered cousin, who suffered from
spinal curvature and dwarfism
both of which kept him in his small chair
in his little room down the hall and like the prophet
he was named for he fell down from his trances
and he was given to Utopian thinking
and lived by an old canal like the first one.

And there was a kind of Warholian laughter
which Andy and I used to resort to
walking across the 7th Street Bridge
now the Warhol Bridge—the Allegheny River—
though there is no Gerald Stern Bridge anywhere
nor Michel Foucault nor Jacques Derrida.

And Hannah Arendt—I'm sure you remember her—
who went back to her lover her teacher in a
peasant's hut in the Black Forest and wept
in his arms as he in hers as he brushed the crumbs
from her Hebrew lips with his Nazi fingers
and published his last explanation in *Der Spiegel*
after his death in 1976.

Bollingen Ezra Pound, 1949

It's a year I remember like no other,
the year I sided with that cold man
and with the committee
and pitied him in his tent
in the hot sun
in the freezing rain
one book only allowed.

It's as if he were locked up in a hotel
and all he had was a Gideon
and he was stuck for a year
in Kings and Ephesians.

Oh to be in England
now that Winston's out
now that there's room for doubt
and the bank shall be the nation's.

Jews, Jews, Jews,
voted against him
and they sold the prize to the least bidder.

Earth receive an honored guest,
lucky those who were laid to rest.

Merwin

The way it was in the eighties
when we carried pockets full of quarters
to give to the destitute
and William ran a whole block south once
to give extra quarters because of the man's dog
a second giving for him
and it was his own Chow he mourned
for weeks on end and how
delighted he was—and shocked—
to see the Chow next door
with his characteristic blue tongue
and his proud and distant way
so that now in the time of no-age
that we share together though across
six hours of land
and six or more of water
I think of him writing in his room full of white light
as our friend Mary Ann describes it
where he's loading his pockets
and he will run down the best he can
to give a second time to the man
with the Border collie though it's more
like a third time now that I think of it.

No One

No one there to remember with me
the election returns of 1931
Hoover losing state after state
Roosevelt getting his speech ready
the first time ever on radio
my father starting to sing in Russian
moving furniture to dance the kazatzka,
nor is there anyone to help me with the words
of a song I sang in Miss Steiner's chorus
nor anyone standing there with me in the blue
rhododendrons or sitting under the blossoms
of my dying redbud, not even brewing
a Kroger tea bag and reading the leaves.

Route 29

This is the place, isn't it?
I parked my car on the shoulder
and walked into the woods
thirty yards to the pool
of water the opposite side
of the canal and the river
the great maples and spruces
sometimes three feet deep
in the freestanding water.

And there is the stretch, isn't it,
where I told an astonished young policeman
I was a professor of police science
when he stopped me one night for weaving.

And this is the time of no time
you get to know in your eighties
reading Paul Goodman and
studying the last poems of Duncan
identical to the typed manuscript
he inscribed for me as a gesture
of love in 1985
at the Pound conference in San Jose
where a door was flung open
in the room where the coats were hung.

Though the canary was red that time
and for a change his name wasn't Dickey
and he flew back into his cage
to get at the calcium,
he who loved horses
and died with his thin legs in the air
and was carried out secretly
to the 1938 Pontiac,
one of the many things
that disappeared around me
since those who first loved me have gone on without me.

Midrash

For Alicia

The women knew the Lord was busy arguing
with the bearded ones in a study house
nor would He ever whisper in a poet's ear
"All is good despite everything."
Not that God.

I don't know if the goyim
knew that Jews put *Him* on trial,
then dragged Him in in chains.
"Well," the Pope said, "at least
they dragged something in, but spitting
was going too far, they wouldn't spit on Him.
Not that God."

And as far as the myth of the good Nazi
is concerned they weren't singing, but praying,
nor would a Nazi guard
ever think of taking the place of a woman.
What? All of them? One of them? He alone?
Nazis are basically good?
They take pity on vermin?
Here's a dead rat with his mouth eaten away.
Kiss it!

Two Boats

I was eating half a chicken and keeping
my head away from the redbud branch that stoops
sometimes to poke me or just to caress me
as well as keeping the sun and wind away,
and sometimes I was Samuel Coleridge and sometimes
Oswald Spengler and I thought if we had
bought the houseboat in 1950 and started
up the Ohio, then down past Steubenville
to Cincinnati and the Mississippi,
how it all would have been radically different
for Donald and me, floating to New Orleans,
but his father never gave him the money and anyhow
he was too boring to live with for such a length
of time—I would have killed him—

                              and if Thanksgiving,
two years later in watery Sète, I had
closed a deal with the French sea captain
to rent a boat and cruise the Mediterranean
from Morocco on the left to Greece on the right
including Crete and Spain and Egypt, six of us,
all students at Montpellier, for what was then
a pittance, I think a thousand dollars a month
simple fare included, that makes a hundred
seventy dollars for each of us, the boat
was built I think when the Phoenicians
founded Carthage, the sail was red, a motor

was added for modernity—but we had our lives
to lead, or so we said, in four
or five cities, including school and jobs
and fiancées—but I have only a drop of
regret, the size of a raindrop that barely escapes
my redbud leaves, I sometimes shake them
to have a little drink, and I have abandoned
Spengler a hundred years ago and now it's
pauvre Spinoza again, he goes with my chicken.

Ravenous

My hands are red from dictionaries
and I suffer from stubbornness and insistence
and my mind is spread out either
under or over this metal table
but I was never a sponger, or a *schnorrer*—
I can tell you that;

but before this day is over
I will finally just eat the
one-thousand-year-old egg
from inside the glass cabinet that
was there for display purposes only,
and unlocked, in the biggest mistake that museum ever made
for I'm a hungry—and curious—raven;

though I'm also a red-billed pigeon
from the densely wooded bottomlands of southernmost Texas
and that's why I'm reading the letters between
Walter Benjamin and Gershom Scholem written at the time of
    the First World War;

and that's why I stopped
putting pencils between the pages of my books
and that's why I have constructed
an imaginary summer house,
the bookcases made of twigs

the roof made from the intertwining branches
of my Japanese maple and my Chinese dogwood
whose red fruit I eat
for eternity's sake on my back porch
nearby the blue-winged madman.

Silence

I once planned a room for pure silence
the walls two feet thick
where I could listen to the Quartets
or just the loose notes floating by.

But I never minded the sound
of Stanley's cornet
mixed as it was
with the sound of the wind
and the shrieks of small birds
blown about over the water.

He, Stan, who stood on his front porch
facing the river
and blasted away at the black locusts
living there.

He—Stan—who borrowed my rowboat
to get a little exercise before he died
just after his displacement and heart attack
and just before Flo's breakdown and suicide.

For he was a D.P. American style,
his retirement stolen one day,
the owner in a cloud somewhere
and twenty-six years of work—
steel for Yankee Stadium and Verrazano Bridge—
gone overnight,

his '53 Dodge truck in the backyard
with its hood up
just like his gold-laden mouth stood open in disbelief,
the grass growing up foot by foot in the dirt around him

for which I added two coats of green wall paint
whose purpose it was to create another layer
of foolproof sound intervention
to keep the grief out.

Dark Blue Geese

There were flocks of blue Canadas
that flew as far south as outside Savannah
that now live, even in December, as far north as the
    Adirondacks.

As across from the cemetery on River Road
is Goose-City where they set up schools, post offices, parks,
T-shirt shoppes, bagelries and jewelries
as in the days of Mayor Koch in Tompkins Square Park
there were hospitals, markets, playgrounds,
schools and massage parlors,

the whole idea being a city inside a city.

At least until the police arrived
and used billy clubs to drive them out
for the park needed to be updated.

Only the Chinese on Avenue A went quietly
abandoning their exercise classes at ten
and their singing at eleven.

The rest protested, especially at the post office and the hospital
for that was the time of marching and rejuvenation.

Ruby Red

Watching a grackle and a cowbird have at it
over an oversize egg though I can't even remember
which state let alone the street and its number
but my box of records comes to mind
I left on the curb along with the TV set
I watched the day of the assassination
and the day after, the murderer and the
murderer murdered in a police station so corrupt
you'd think it was a small town in rural Mississippi
and not the fifth largest, site of museums,
universities and theaters, where the Rubensteins lived
a dentist, a teacher, and a small-time crook, gofer, and killer
I learned about in Punxsutawney, PA
only it was only visible
when the poem made it visible though
it was raining and there wasn't a dry leaf in sight,
Sunday, November 24th, 1963.

A Walk Back from the Restaurant

How fitting it was to see a fat and evil cat
in the dirt and dead leaves of a cement pot
next door to the Presbyters, the same self-righteous
bastards that moved dear Robbie Burns in his
modest apologia, "Holy Willie's Prayer,"
the single best poem of 1785,
and try to figure out which century the wood trim
and railings and such were last painted
and who the old woman was who lived there with her twenty cats
and how many years ago her loving husband died in his sleep
and how—and if at all—it was possible to disentangle
we'd have to probe the ultimate secret again
since the in-your-face and self-congratulating mayor
couldn't, in spite of his bulk and his slanted forehead, help us
     with that.

Lips

Sitting with his friends he learned how shameful it was
to have played the golden trombone and not the wooden flute
and to have blasted his own way into manhood that way
instead of making a soft sound with his mouth and fingers.

But he was stubborn and anyhow he had thick lips
which stood him in good stead in one case but not the other,
and furthermore his friends had died,
one two three, one after another.
And he was left to his own devices,
I would say his own instruments.

He could have considered a harp, or, in his case, a lyre
and found a tall stool to display his wares,
I haven't forgotten that,
for he wasn't—finally—restricted to one thing.
Indeed a mouth organ if push came to shove,
something he could almost swallow for the drama's sake.

Think of him getting rid of spit
and warming up behind the French horns,
the French horns he hated beyond anything
for their thin lips and their benevolent sounds.

Main Bridge

I was practically inside a cave underneath the main bridge
and first I studied the struts, then the bolts, then the
rust—which I loved so dearly—just above me.
I don't think the cave bear lived here
though honey, eggs, wild carrots, onions, and
baby rabbits were in easy reach.
Most of the noise was from vehicular traffic
though the wooden roof bore witness to horses and sometimes
    wagons.

It was a great place to read Hart Crane
and Dylan Thomas, but just after our late lunch
since it got dark there first.

Pittsburgh Sun-Telegraph, 1939

The one thing that kept me going above all else
were the potatoes we roasted in the burning ash
and for their sake I made one trip too many
on the three-bladed sled.

I was the one with the salt shaker which I wrapped in wax paper
and stuffed into my jacket pocket.

I still had three newspapers left
but they were of no use since the edges
of the front sections were brown already and curled
so we paid no attention to the melt
which had already started in southern Ohio
and was working its way quickly across West Virginia
and Pennsylvania, since they always reported the weather on
    page one
and that information was burnt to a crisp.

Ritsos

They thought if they cut off one finger at a time
he would stop his complaining,
but he buried his work in laundry baskets and refrigerators
and sang, as the blue jay does,
at the top of his voice.

They removed a lung
but he transferred his breath to his kidney
and died from stuffing too much music
into one of his lobes, I forget which.

Bohème

Just as in the birth of Venus there were bivalvers
twenty years before and twenty years after the painting,
I was there at the birth of the modern
though I wouldn't be born until twenty years later.

After deformation I went in for superimposed planes
but I always ate lunch with Max Jacob
so as not to get too technical about it.

He was the one who got himself a job
through his cousin sweeping floors in the family department store
and delivering purchases in a wheelbarrow and shared
his putrid earnings with Picasso in the early days.

Women hate Picasso but they once loved him
as I do sometimes since I identify with his
very last work where he kept a certain distance,
looked down with horror and resorted to myth
as he moved away from the lyricism of the early paintings.

Decades

With me, it wasn't a yellow cab
but an orange streetcar going 40 mph
on a hillside through the woods and everything
shaking and rattling and through a short tunnel
slightly lit by dim blue lights a seat for
the conductor, a kind of throne I sometimes sat on
and that makes two things gone this morning, I'm only
counting for obsession's sake, I thought of
the card we put in the living room window, "ice"
it said on one side, "coal" the other, but I've
done that already, how about making colored
fans and selling them door to door, how about
being a helper and shoveling the dirty coal
down the chutes at 25 cents an hour—
I have to check if anyone else has done this,
one of my upstate or New England friends,
I loved to watch men working, I loved to sit
and eat with them, and see them smoke and listen
to them talk, they were my first prophets.

Those Who Loved Budapest

In those years what divided us was
those who loved the plaques and those who didn't
and those with amour on their lips
and those who rode up the forty-six floors
and climbed the thirty-six steps
to look down on the little lives
and compare them to their own
and those who worshipped Hegel
for his dialectics
and those who insisted on water
especially a river that
it was possible to swim across
in addition to watching the sun setting
in the steep hills the other side
and those who took a train to England
with others their same age
seventy-six years ago
and those who found
a filthy orange bathtub in the rubble
and those who found a French porcelain candlestick
or Eckermann's *Conversations* in perfect condition
on top of Byron's *Poems*
and those who loved Budapest and those who didn't.

Gold

It may sound crazy but I left my dedicated bench
to follow a quick-moving English sparrow
along with a shiny starling on top of her
down a narrow path surrounded on both sides
by American poison, something that doesn't exist
in either England or, for that matter, France,
altering forever the habit of outdoor living

but the birds had nothing to say—or do—
of any importance unless it was to point out
our corrupt history as revealed on the copper plate
attached to the granite base of Tilden's statue,

he who was cheated out of the presidency
by the machinations of Rutherford B. Hayes,
he who rested his left hand on the Constitution
while signing checks with his right for the new library

but there are no doves
and the tree does not replenish itself
nor is there an ancient woman to talk to
for the kind of gold we have only blackens the hand.

The One in Paris

I wrapped the paperweight in an old undershirt
and almost ran past Goldenberg's, too
happy, maybe too excited, to stop for
my piece of herring and my black bread;

I climbed two steps at a time
to show my wife
to whom I pointed out again and again
the smooth glass pressing down on the red
and yellow flowers and turned the piece this way and that
to look for imperfections or just to admire
the beauty in the morning sunlight and plan
where we would put it, either on the wobbly
green table or on top of the chifforobe,

but we would still save the river stones
for they came from the Delaware
nor did we know what they were called in French
nor could we find it in our small French dictionary,
some pages of which I had torn out for notes,

and that summer there was so much wind
we put it to its proper use, which Aristotle
would have admired as is evidenced by
his testimony in both *The Ethics* and *The Physics*,
and I came to believe it came from the court

of Charlemagne though my wife insisted
on India or Byzantium for she was a
serious student of glass at the time,
as well as book binding I might add,
and now I'm looking for a millennial
to give it to for preservation
is the kind of love I'm now addicted to.

Ecstasy

The reason broken glass wouldn't do
it was stolen from a Norwegian novel of the same name,
the movie by that name starred Hedy Lamarr,
the most beautiful woman in Europe
running naked through a forest in Bavaria.

It's to be repossessed, a strange word
that has to do with Toyotas and Chevys.
It's at least a kind of dislocation
or, as Ira says, a boundless absorption of the world.

I see it as an abandonment of self, as if the white horse
who dove sixty feet into the ring of fire did it
of his own accord and the rider with her spurs
was merely sitting there and thinking how the water in that tank
would not flow into the holes of her face this time
the ears the eyes the large mouth the two noses.

Book of the Dead

You take yourself sitting there
only in the fall this time
waiting for nothing to happen,
just listening more than anything else
and shocking yourself to hear how noisy it is
and trying to identify the low rumble
that's here as much as it is on an island on Broadway
with dedicated benches and small flower gardens,
only here there's a train whistle
and a kind of dull clanging from across the river
that belongs more to the outer reaches than the inner,
and when I open my eyes
there's a golden leaf on my page
with black patches and real holes on one side
the other a kind of lime green
with more imperfect leaves
waiting their turn
the floor thick with them.

The Year of Everything

It was while he was collapsing under the weight of
the chifforobe that he considered inner and outer things
though at the moment inner was his pain and outer was
him at the other end in addition to the chifforobe itself.

He used to think of balance, harmony it could be
called, with maybe a slight tilt inward as if he were
moving his mind east ah gradually and even considering
the lotus and some straw to sleep on instead of the hairy

mattress and spring and headboard it would be impossible
to carry up Iron Mountain or Black or Red or Ragged,
whatever his fancy was and wherever his harmony took him,
and, as he said to his green Honda, it was only the body of
   Bliss he was

after, never mind "body," never mind that "bliss," a word
too close to happiness, ecstasy, something either
vague or unearned, though he at last had grown fearless
when it comes to languor and even provoked himself

as he did here with philosophical debate and a kind of
wordage he would have called too discursive when
he was twenty-five or thirty but he did what he did
and he praised the year he wrote his new book of poems

even if it was a year of murder and ignorance
talk about outer things, talk about the world
as opposed to the self and the name he gave
it was the year of everything.

Billionaires

So what if it wasn't a weeping beech
three hundred years old blotting out the mountains
one way, the ocean the other; what if
it was only a fig (only a fig, he says!)
given over to bareness every few years
and soon, up here, to be covered in plastic
like a Hasid wife hidden from the world
of hunger and thirst for those of us who go about with
buckets, eating our profits up, wheezy and fig-laden.

Thanks to the Sicilians for bringing the fig tree here
and thanks to the Dutch for planting the weeping beech
for in 1714 neither the Germans nor the Poles had arrived
and there were very few gardens with potatoes and cabbages
though there were so-called English who later changed their
    loyalties
but not one fig tree till 1910 or so,
brought over a mere baby from Palermo on a steamship
that stopped first in Naples, then in Glasgow before
it came to New York, Hell's Kitchen then Queens,
then in the 1970s Long Island
in Mattituck, this to continue the cultivation
begun 10,000 years ago in Jericho
on the North Fork close to the alligator's back teeth
if you look at a map of eastern Long Island
shaped, as it is, like an alligator's open mouth,

the Hamptons too expensive for such a beast,
his lower jaw rolling in dough.

Two Things

Always it's putting two things together
that don't necessarily belong there,
Dizzy Dean of the St. Louis Cardinals
calling in his outfield and striking out
the last three Pittsburgh Pirates to win
a crucial game at Forbes Field—and the
bombing of Addis Ababa by Count Ciano
the son-in-law of Benito Mussolini
who described the destruction in terms of lovely blossoms
spreading out in the smoke of the lower atmosphere.

The year was 1936 and my father,
driving a 1935 silver-gray Pontiac,
described the Ethiopians sitting on the heads
of African elephants, carrying poisonous spears
which would destroy the Fascists using outmoded weapons
from World War I too terrified to do battle
with Ethiopia—Abyssinia it was called,
a great empire which had resisted Mohammed
and *his* son-in-law 1,500 years earlier
and everything before and after since Sheba.

I also have a vague memory of the hood ornament
I think it was an Indian "chieftain"
with a dour puss as it was on old nickels
as I remember, and for all I know there's a stamp

with a feather or two, most likely turkey
but it could be goose or even crow but never
canary and never for that matter parrot,
so accurate the artists at GM were
whether they were designing the hood ornaments
of Chevys or Cadillacs, which I also remember,

for without knowing it I was an expert on many things
especially baseball cards and stamps and I had one of
Honus Wagner and a few gorgeous French Empires
which surpassed I thought those of the English since
if the sun never set on the British Empire
it did set on their artisans at least when it came to
stamps, it was a Martinique
I especially loved, the upright tits
and—in spite of the gender—the bolo knife that cut
its way through the forests as if the trees were butter

which brings up the great subject and what
an eleven-year old was doing admiring tits,
especially the pointed kind that began
higher on the upper body than nature
allowed maybe with a tiny baby sucking
or one on her mother's back too small anatomically
all of which got him started at an early age
hunting through magazines for undressed women

and trading in flutter-books, his favorite the goings-on
between Bluto and Olive, Wimpy and Geezil watching

I could compare to flying the friendly skies
of newnited with a hit on cattle cars and a
boughten sandwich, this way bringing together
what doesn't at first (and second) blush belong there
which you might call a metaphoric rage
for we are used to that where like is more and
I have a pen with an eraser my darling
and you are a 1940 radio and
you are seventeen inches of snow in Michigan
shall I compare thee to a winter's day?

Larry

He kept a hog in Utah
as big as an old bathroom
and parked it in his parlor
so he could polish one bristle at a time

and he kept a horse in his heart
a capacious meadow surrounding him,
the one with a holy ankle,
nor did he forget the bruised jockey.

And he missed my war
though he had a good one of his own
for which he wrote the best poem known
of the alphabetized corpses

and suffered Ike only as a boy
and never took the ride
to Sète on a French bicycle
and staggered back home in the French moonlight.

I had the great honor of introducing him to New Orleans
and watching him jump with joy oh literally
as we visited Hebrew Rest for sorrow
and the caves on Bourbon for cold beer

and we both loved the same woman years apart,
and it was I who called her up
to give her the bad news to which she said
"Now I'm going upstairs to read every word he ever wrote."

Les Fleurs

We ate flowers then
to prolong our lives;
I first read it in Empson,
Seven Types of Ambiguity

Though he knew how banal it was,
the number 7, as "the square of seven,"
"the 7th floor," "7th heaven,"
"7 come 11."

He wanted to do 8
but the truth was he didn't

and I had to sit in the little park
on 106th in the dark

reading "Byzantium"
and "Sailing to Byzantium"

by Y,
Y himself—

> How can I, that girl standing there,
>   My attention fix
>   On Roman or on Russian
>   Or on Spanish politics?

oh God,
pass me a columbine.

Never Again

I'm sneezing too much now and my nose runs a lot
and the swallowing has come back after seventy years
but in the meantime I'm sticking to flowers
rather than meatballs say or dead fish;

and if a mule gets there first
we'd have to shoot craps
or maybe play nine ball and you know
how bad a mule can be at that

so here's a red rose for you
I'll just have a dandelion
garnished with green grass,
but not a grandfather
for you fooled me once with white hair
but never again.

Croissant Moon

If it weren't for the crescent moon what would there be
for lovers—well, if the sky was black or even
studded they could lean back or lie down
as in a planetarium and just point things
out especially a plane that looked like a star
two million miles away on its descent
to a runway although those days it didn't
just sit in the sky for a while and then hurl down,
to Idlewild say, when there was still an Idlewild
and all of western Long Island was more primitive,
more human, fewer people, more
trees, more space for lovers, moon or not,
shaped like a croissant or not, although nearby,
where I buy them, fat and round
with nothing of the crescent in them, as far as
shape, as if in a crescent moon
there was nothing crescent there but just some lumpish
dough as if the love itself could disappear—ah,
we were lucky, there still was love,
there still was a crescent moon, there still was endearment.

Hope Mountain

I was a good city block up from
the stones down there—I think I was on Grant Street
though going out of town most of the streets aren't named
and I looked down longingly yet I wondered if
I turned left would I
be free of grief and was there a fiddler somewhere
since four cut strings were hanging
over a stone and were they snapped or was
the fiddle smashed in the end or was it such on
that hill and in that empty valley, was it
such that they only grieved for each other since it
was so silent there, did Smith grieve for Fox did William
and Mary grieve for Charles Mulroney, did Reba
Guanieri grieve for Rabbi Sandy and if it
came to that would they smash my Bluesband silver harmonica?

To Comfort You

In the beginning was bear scat
so I guess that bears were there before coyotes
not to mention how different the smells are.

But he certainly wasn't enthroned
nor did he have a chariot—
neither of them did—except the bear did rise up
on his hind legs to comfort you,
the way a crocodile would
or a St. Bernard to show you were brothers,

I love that there was no legerdemain;
if he did do something amazing to the darkness
or if he snapped his teeth like a tuning fork
on his way to grab some berries
as coyote did on his way to grab a rabbit
he didn't bullshit while on the path—
or bearshit either.

There is no question he was heterodox;
God himself gave up eating red meat
and that's why the Temple priests were so pissed
he ate a little chicken and a little fish, that's all,
some Brussels sprouts and sweet potatoes too.

The bear tried once to separate himself from the world
and lived inside an enormous dead tree for over a year
but that didn't work too well;
for one thing he couldn't cut back on sugar
even though he was unattached.
He was lacking, he said, because of his sloping shoulders
and though he was stronger than a bull for that matter,
he was sloped.

Thieves and Murderers

That was when I was reading Villon
and fell in love forever
with thieves and murderers
so long as they could rhyme in Latin and French,
but not long after forever I changed again
though I didn't want to become too Eisenhowerish,
he who fell under the desk
at the first sign of a bomb,
he who made love to his driver and, as I remember,
was scolded by George Marshall
and a little later made his maiden speech
at Columbia where he was being "prepared"
for what's good for Raisin Bran is good for America.

Days on end I watched Orson Welles and his company
rehearse *Macbeth* in a small French church
somewhere on the other bank
which stood him in good stead
after he returned to the land of his fathers, my uncles.

I was back to thieves and murderers then
where there were strings galore
and odes and dirges on the first and second floor,
old PA 611
where the flying fishes play

and the dawn comes up like thunder
out of China cross the bay.

Talking Angels

We were talking angels, Willis and I,
and he went back again and again to the
fallen angels—as in Milton—for he was
at heart a sans-culotte, the reason he started
writing poems in French in the first place,
and though I loved Beelzebub and the names in Enoch
and the long lists in Cabala and Apocryphal,
still, at my age, it was more to the point
to get in touch—if that's the word—with Azrael,
stationed as he was in the third heaven,
or someone else carrying the book that day
writing down and erasing names constantly,
whatever being in the book means,
though Anne Marie says you've done enough
and quit following anyone with a thick pen
sticking out of his pocket and loose pages
dropping into the river but Willis and I
both know the last will be first
as we both know the new names may not count
for they may have been bestowed by a two-bit flunky
as my grandfather's was on *Elitz* Island
and what the spelling of my family name was
in the stinking village they came from
and what the name of the village itself was
it's in dispute among the forty-four cousins,
that is, the ones still breathing.

Mad Ireland Drove Him into Poetry

It could just as well have been
the Spanish Flu or the Potato Famine
or maybe just boredom.

For Roethke and Kunitz on old 611
it was the father—in one case, abandonment,
the other, oppression.

In my case—so I think—
it was the lack of a wall
let alone a desk or a chest of drawers or a radio,
as it was a dead sister
and a melancholic mother.

But most of all it was the Murphy bed,
although it was the message I got one day
from a blue jay as large as a crow and beautiful
to boot, who ate small frogs and hated cardinals

and one from squirrels and dogs
and one from opossums and one from groundhogs,
and once from a beetle and once from a worm
fat to bursting

who was eating me already—though we were friends—
and ended up pulling each other out of the wet ground
and holding on to the underground rocks and rootlets
for balance.

Prince of the Second Heaven

Who the angel of February is
I can't remember
though I do know the angel of July
so I'll spend a day with Gustav Davidson
going through his alphabets
for I have things to say
since the angel changes when you reach ninety,
and isn't it fine that I'll remember
while tying my shoes or making my bed?

In Andalucía six of the saints,
though they may have done their serious work
as early as their forties or even thirties
lasted well into their nineties
which I never forgot
when I walked through their cities.

It's mainly Judah Halevi I think about
and his brutal death his first day in Jerusalem
when he was in his early sixties
and the poems he would have written
into his ninetieth
or even six years later
when he was approaching a hundred.

I like his love poems the most
when he forgot the burden
that Moishe placed on him.
Moishe who went up alone
and came back by himself
with only his own testimony
when it says endlessly
there must be two witnesses
and they themselves must be credible,
he even killed alone.

Dirty Music

The way we celebrated we ate
liverwurst sandwiches on rye bread
smeared with Hellmann's
after banging on pots and pans
till two in the morning—keeping time
to the broken furnace only a foot below us,
Muriel singing arias to Italian operas
Basara pounding a cardboard box
Noël sawing a broom in half
to make some sticks but converting to
the whistling saw itself, Louise clapping spoons
and singing love songs from the Second War,
me with my Bluesband harmonica
Pat pregnant, sleeping it off upstairs.

Sunset

At the horizon line there was a touch of pink
but everything above was a heavy gray with
streaks of white behind it though yesterday it
was two black lines stretching across the sky with
the red then the pink behind it but it wasn't the
end of days, it was just two variations
showing through the slightly moving palm trees

but I wasn't sure that a madman wouldn't ride down the
street on a large white horse with a sword hanging
from his mouth murdering left and right with ten
million angels shouting after him or twenty
million monkeys as the sages of India have it,
all with harmonicas and pocketknives loving
Apocalypse, as they called it, given the darkness.

Coal Barons

What she was doing there in the first place
was resting her tired back after the journey
from Lexington to Park and so on
and sat herself down first on one of the stones
guarding a building and then on one of the chairs
in the theater district in the designated space
for the weary of spine—at last—though she would call it
exhausted of hearts for everything in New York
becomes transformed into something else
and it is that something else we love to die for

and like a weeping garland she will end up in
a clown's suit which I knew a little from wearing
a crepe disguise going from house to house
collecting apples with razor blades inside them
and dumping it all on the kitchen table coughing my
lungs out from the filthy air and the journey
itself begging for Mars bars and cashews
since I was finally a pirate in crepe as my son
was a corpse in a coffin his mother and her friend
made from a cardboard box painted black
and he was heavily powdered such that the neighbors
were horrified for he was only seven
and knocked on the doors alone or with his friends
in his shocking costume fifty miles east of Pittsburgh
where the coal barons, dressed up as miners

with lights on their heads and cages of canaries
most of them dead mostly named Dickey their
legs in the air, the barons blowing whistles,
oh those barons they loved it, they loved
it, it was the rich in rags
imitating the poor, it's what they did,

no, it's what they *do*, they help each other
into the rotten clothes, they stop to look at
themselves in mirrors they live in fake humility
they carry their lunches in in rusty tin lunch boxes.

Orson

Orson Welles has been my philosopher
for the last few weeks now and if he's just a
phenomenon and doesn't really have a system
as Spinoza did or Anaxagorus, he
at least is consistent even if some of the things
he talks about are immensely unimportant
except to actors maybe or gossipmongers.

It was 1950—I think—in a Protestant church
near the Pont d'Austerlitz we met him directing
a small troupe in *Macbeth* even before he
made the movie; he was taking a vacation
from America during the naming of names and I had
the honor not only of watching them rehearse
but having some *vin ordinaire* afterwards.

Of the poets, it was Dylan Thomas he seemed to
love the most and just because I could speak
one poem after another he assumed
I was a tub-thumper myself though it was Stevens—
an English edition—and Hopkins I carried around
and hateful Pound I dragged from place to place
and Crane, his ecstasy.

As far as God
Orson, like every secularist, was evasive
and spoke of unknown gases and random objects
floating through the universe and called what was called
sin just selfishness—this from a heavyweight
eating his steaks and potatoes at 2 or 3 a.m.
the No. 1 saint of the sinners of old Hollywood.

Visit from Mars

Nostradamus generally predicted the
future but he also shined a clear
light into the past and lived to
regret some of the visions he had
because they weren't precise enough
and could have been used for nefarious
thoughts or perilous judgments since,
after all, he *was* a prophet though
he could have been called a false
prophet in the sense that both
Ezekiel and Isaiah speak of them
though I have to say that
he predicted the visit from Mars, orchestrated
by Orson Welles in 1938
in the town of Grover's Mill, near Princeton
where everyone seemed to turn on
the radio five, ten, minutes after the
show started including my father and
mother who were packing suitcases
for a quick ride to the bluff
and a cave my father knew from
his early years nor did he ever
forgive Orson Welles for the broadcast
and wouldn't talk to me about *Touch of
Evil*—the greatest—nor *Citizen Kane,*
mostly a little boring though

if you were a film buff you could
study it forever especially if
you hated Hearst for all the good reasons.
Einstein himself was interviewed
while walking the mulberry streets, especially
the right-hand side of Great Road, going south,
where the houses are windy and overpriced,
and he was full of denial that anyone
with a radio antenna sticking out of his head
had been seen in any diner or hardware store,
Einstein whose bushy face had rubbed
many a pair of reddened lips,
Einstein whose famous name they stole for bagels.

Gelato

The two nuns I saw I urged them to
convert to Luther or better yet to join
the Unitarians, and the Jews I
encountered to think seriously about
Jesus, especially the Lubavitchers,
and I interrupted the sewer workers
digging up dirt to ask them
how many spoonfuls of sugar they
put in their coffee and the runners in
their red silk to warn them about
the fake fruit in their yogurt since
to begin with I was in such a good
mood this morning waiting patiently
for the two young poets driving over from
Jersey City to talk about the late forties
and what they were to me when I was their age and
we turned to Chinese poetry and Kenneth Rexroth's
Hundred Poems and ended up
talking about the Bollingen and Pound's
stupid admiration of Mussolini
and how our main poets were on the right
politically—most of them—unlike the European
and South American and we climbed some steps
into a restaurant I knew to buy gelato
and since we were poets we went by the names,
instead of the tastes and colors—and I stopped talking

and froze beside a small tree since I was
older than Pound was when he went silent
and kissed Ginsberg, a cousin to the Rothschilds,
who had the key to the ghetto in his pocket,
one box over and two rows up, he told me.

Ancient Chinese Egg

I counted wrong in the other poem,
it was five hundred years, not a thousand
so that meant the egg was cooked
during the time of Ben Jonson, it also
was neither simmered nor steamed, but baked
in the sun on the heated rocks, I'd say three minutes
in the way we keep time in this era and since I
"obtained" it in 1970 it had to be
the grandson, and the poets were late Ming
and one of them wrote about the swarm of flies
on his sick horse and what the smell of blood was
and one of them wrote about his *pauvre* hut in the mountains
as if it were still early T'ang but what the hell,
a hut is a hut be it this be it that
and self-pity in terms of the geese coming north
is the same both here and there, the egg on the outside
was perfect though I'm a little nervosa
of what I'd find inside so I tossed it
from hand to hand stopping once or twice
to read and reread the certificate
of priceless possession and how I could reduce
the value to zero by just two gulps,
or a few nibbles at the parameters;
ah, one of them wrote of his life
wasted on Weights and Measures and how his shoes
were ruined by the time he got home for he couldn't carry

them swinging from side to side
while he walked barefoot the thousand miles
for he was too old and soft and had a wattle
under his chin—he'd have to stop
dozens of times,
and consider that though the Manchu regime was coming,
in Europe it was no better
though since it was almost June he still could be saved
by the tragic solitary dark red iris
forcing its way again through the dense green hedges.

Loneliness

Nothing by or for itself, the sound of
eggs hard-boiling in the hot water
echoed by the heavy rain that pours
down the broken spout, the cowardly lion's
roar answered by the moos of the buffalo
the bloody mouth of the one
by the sharp and polished horns of the other,
even Nelson Eddy
could hear someone else singing in his bathtub
the songs from his dumb movies

though when I once drove up the vertical highway
in Colorado to visit Elaine the Gnostic
and take her to the stone mountain
where her husband fell
we drove back without talking
though she touched my knee in gratitude and when
we reached the very top there were no trees
only flowers grew there
accompanied by nothing
the name of which was loneliness
which Shelley the poet himself suffered from
among his beleaguered women
you'll die remembering.

Hamlet Naked

It was a theater west on 47th
that smelled inside of urine
both upstairs and down,
you wouldn't believe it
but it was *Hamlet* naked, not *Lear*, not love
next door to where ten or so men
were facing the walls and swaying
in what was called a bookstore
across the street from Nedick's, orange soda and hot dogs
for which I'll say just this
that some could bend their knees while swaying
and move their lips
and shut their books with a loud Amen.

When I walked east past Broadway
I hesitated too long and by this act
I had to press the button twice to change
the red to green, for I was in a fog,
and someone should light a bonfire
since I could walk wherever I wanted then
and didn't know north from south or east from west
nor was it Papp *his* Hamlet circa
1968 nor Dante naked nor Faust,
it was instead your normal lewdness
posing in a halfhearted way as art.

I was ironic then as I am now
but my head was too far down as if I were looking
for nickels, though anything less than a quarter
I wouldn't disgrace myself.
Maybe I was looking at the metal doors
open to let the light down into the cellar,
Gregory Corso playing the harmonica,
Diana Trilling with a toy cello,
both I saw one day on Avenue A
among the bags of rice and the boxes of lettuce,
the old Ukrainian restaurant which this late date
could be an expensive Armenian or Ethiopian,
diners sucking it up with chunks of bread
for there is nothing but improvement now
among the lettered streets, and there was a learned
couple with a five-year-old, all three had
matching neckties—I want to wear one
when I go into the cellar, I want to be
arrested for causing havoc, especially when a
crowd gathers around the opening—
in New York a crowd can form in a second, think
of Gregory, a blue jay on his head,
think of Diana seeing a live rat,
think of me lying on the gunnysacks
            my left arm up
            conducting.

Believe It

Of Miami Beach I know a ton
for I drank coconut milk
in the year Wendell Wilkie
ran against FDR.

I would do a sidearm pitch with my coconut
if I only knew the name of the hotel
where we were the first.

I could smell the new wood in my room
my white ducks with a perfect crease my short sleeves
my coconut going 120 mph.

What struck me then—and now—were the cafeterias
only in the South they had the grown-up male children of ex-slaves
to carry your tray to your table, above their heads
New York too the Jews had cafeterias only no slaves
and that's why they felt at home in all that Drecko
and on the beach where they sang in Yiddish and danced in the
    sand.

You should see me and Sonny Uncles walking at night in the
    cold water
singing "Moon Over Miami," piece of corn, piece of dreck,
you should see her teaching me to kiss
under a royal palm the sound of the waves taking over,

better by a long shot than the empty beaches and the
    expensive apartments
of Rat's Mouth.

Believe it!

KGB, The Reading

I despised the KGB not only for its name
but for the two long sets of stairs you had to climb
and for the room where different cultures met
one for poetry, one just for standing and drinking
so you had to guess the noises where you belonged
and when you read there was the murmur
the periodic fake scream or the shout
nor did they give you even a beer for your efforts
never an envelope stuffed with cash
and never a check with Chase at the top or Bank of
America you opened with a pencil first the carbon
then the yellow wood you secretly read
spying on yourself oh in a men's room
with piss on the floor and neither hot air nor paper
towel in sight the window barred you couldn't
go feet first onto a flat roof
and climb down somewhere to freedom even jumping
the last five feet you knew how to bend your
knees and cushion the fall you had the courage
to leave you even walked down the two sets of stairs
holding on to the dirty wall and smiling at
the latecomers I'll be back in a minute you
said or I'm just going round the corner
to have a plate of spaghetti find a seat
or stand on the table to look at the paintings
hold your breath tie your shoes, the moon

did you notice is almost full what's that called?
Have a glass of wine I'll have a margarita,
just a little salt, I have some books
near where I'll be sitting, buy one and get
used to my rhythms read Larry Levis and
Deborah Digges they were lovers, I knew "The
Bridge" by heart have you read "Tusks of Blood"
by Samuel Greenberg maybe the greatest poem
of the twentieth century.

Goldfinches

Seventy-two degrees outside when we
walked past Sutter's Gate nor could we say
what made the sky that color though someone
said it was dust and we found a bench we liked
going south a mile or so and we just rested and
didn't say a word to our neighbors among the plantings
nor did we count the windows on either side
and just for once we let
the goldfinches do the flying.

Marriage Song

What if there were rain on one side and sun on the other
Is that why you came?

Would you sit on a rock overlooking the sea
        and wait for a disturbance?
Would there be the green moss underneath, the wetness you love,
        or would there be doves,
        one more or less white, one speckled?

Is that why you took the wooden causeway
that only rose one foot over the water
and went through the swamp where the boa constrictor
        makes its new life?

Would you reach a hand out to tempt the alligator?
Who took the coin when your mother crossed over?
How long will you pine?

West Virginia

Who knows what happens in the
last dregs of the mason jar?
And where you put the thumb
and what the left shoulder does

and what good the maps were
for I was crazy for maps
and likewise crazy to go to the wilds
but there were no wilds in the places I thought of

and I was already in touch with a realtor
and one of my questions was the fate of the Jews
though I knew the history by heart:
someone named Cohen came by on a mule

with buttons ribbons needles and scissors
and the first synagogue was in Wheeling
and one of the mules became a department store
and after a while there were ten mules

and one beard was thick and curly
the other was thin and straw-colored
and both loved the old rivers
before the Cock brothers came by to drain them.

I think you place the right thumb
in the small round handle and press the jar
against your clavicle while tilting your head back
converting to philosophy ecstasy and drunkenness.

Fall 1960

Castro himself—you won't believe it—ate Wheaties
for breakfast at his hotel in Harlem
I remember it was the Theresa and they
cooked chickens in the kitchen they brought over
from Cuba for they were afraid John Foster Dulles
or his brother Allen Dulles might poison them
and Khrushchev took off his heavy black shoe and turned on
the radio at 4:45 to hear the
latest adventure of Jack Armstrong, the All-
American Boy and I even stopped
kissing my close friend's wife while he was in the bathtub
soaking, drunk and singing songs from the islands
off Messina, he who worked for the Quakers
and was fired for drinking and singing, though soaking
was acceptable, here is the song:
    We the Piper Hudson High Boys
    show them how we stand,
    never tired of Wheaties,
    the best food in the land
    so won't you try Wheaties
    the best breakfast food in the land.

Mulberries

I had to eat my way to freedom
since I was the only non-bird who
ate them instead of sucking down the Tylenol
at least in May the Northern and Southern regions
where I spent most of my childhood sliding.

My mouth was red, my face was blue
my hands were filthy my shoes were caked.
It was the Psalter mainly but also Exodus
where Moishe slid down Sinai
and broke a bone.

Three cheers for mulberries
and the purple fruit we add to our briskets
and the fritters most of all we cook in lard
and sugar and rum and flour.

Three cheers for the queen of cookbooks
who slid in Venice
as I did once
and almost broke her hip.

Philadelphia, North of Huntingdon

Who knows what I told you?
The main thing was Logan, now
crowded with boarded-up windows and square nails and crows
where one store sold only butter and cheese
and another eggs, where a thin man in a black suit
and speckled underwear
sat in a chair and candled the eggs
then boxed the good one,

and the birthday party of the Russian next door
who had dozens of starched white shirts in his closet
all facing the same way, and whose wife
put a bottle of vodka beside every plate
at the table which stretched through two rooms of
that tiny house exactly like ours with a little rail
between the two, and three worn wooden steps
in front of each and the singing and crawling over the
rail, drunk after the dark had set in
and the nightjars were warming up,

and the long talk with the crow who cawed me well
and I just criticized though she said I was wrong,
they were *cleaning* the earth while we
were defiling it

but after a while we flew
to the nearest branch since I was accommodating
her though I didn't go so far as learning
a language, and kissing, I have no idea,
sixty years later what that part of the city
is like now and if I were there
I certainly wouldn't find one egg nor would it be
worthwhile, I think, to improve it, who wants
to put a new rail in and paint it, who
wants to drink vodka with a bunch of
crazy Rooskies anyhow, who wants to
look under everything in order to find a crow?

My Grave

It was the quartz that gave you hope
digging two stories down in the underworld
though I called it glass and dragged
my children in to see the bright sparks.

Two hours east there was glass in the wet sand
to harden the sidewalks
and there was glass too, wasn't there,
in the arms and legs you carried.

During the long life we may have swallowed a bit
from the broken peanut butter jars
but I go back always to the dirt I was shoveling out
beneath that ancient house.

Not Romania, not Hungary,
but Pennsylvania where I was caught for a second
with my arms in the air,
my small shovel enlarging

a concealed space
though some around me
with smiling lips
called it my grave.

Skylark

That's my suit Johnny Mercer is wearing,
the buttonhole at top visible through the lapel,
the jacket loose the hands falling
naturally in the trouser pockets,
the look required one of disdain what you'd call
arrogance for want of a better word,
a joke Hoagy Carmichael told him
still in his smile, the words to "Skylark"
in his inside breast coat pocket,
honeysuckle everywhere, everywhere,
the main lie of the thirties and forties, the last
century, the one I was born in.

The Other

I woke up determined to turn everything
upside down, to convert music to protest
and protest to song,

always struggling against the Other

and there was a baby robin on the ground
screaming just to unnerve me and—
more—there was its mother in the Japanese
Maple half-scolding, half-beseeching,
all this to bring me to my knees
to unhold myself from the screwed-in 2×4
where I was doing one leg at a time to strengthen
my back and stomach muscles and I discovered
again the Other could be the mother or the
baby, or even the tree itself.

One War

It was a shame that I had only one war
and one pair of leather boots.

Left right left
you had a good home and you left
there ain't no use in lookin' round
there ain't no discharge on the ground.

Sound off, one two
one two—three four.

It was a shame that there was only a night bird
to welcome me home.

And a shame I threw my barracks bag
into the river.

And shame there weren't two hundred other bags
to float on the oil.

A shame I had to wait for forty minutes
for the No. 6 on Second Avenue
and listen to the goatsucker when I only wanted to hear the
    wild canary.